READINGS
IN
ANGLICAN
SPIRITUALITY

COMPILED BY

DAVID HEIN

FORWARD MOVEMENT PUBLICATIONS
CINCINNATI

David Hein was educated at St. Paul's School (Brooklandville, Maryland) the University of Virginia, and the University of Chicago. Since 1983 he has taught in the religion and philosophy department of Hood College, Frederick, Maryland.

—— Contents ——

—INTRODUCTION—

No book can substitute—in immediacy, vitality, and sensitivity—for a personal relationship. An insightful colleague, a sage spiritual director, a thoughtful friend will have known you over time, will see you as a distinct individual, and thus should be able to respond to you in a way that is dynamic rather than static.

While marks on paper can never replace that kind of encounter, it is also true that the relation between reader and text is not a static one, either, and that the printed word possesses its own unmistakable companionability. There are authors in this volume who have been friends to generation after generation, who have spoken to all sorts and conditions of men and women, and who somehow retain the capacity to say the fitting thing here and now.

The present collection may not include your own favorite writer on spiritual matters. Today's Episcopalians read Thomas Merton and Henri Nouwen (Church of Rome) with as much fervor as they imbibe Austin Farrer and C.S. Lewis (Church of England). And you would certainly be correct to point out that English spirituality itself actually comprises a far richer and more variegated set of works than is represented in these pages. It rests upon the Old and New Testaments, the church fathers, and The Book of Common Prayer, and includes such figures as Anselm of Canterbury, Julian of Norwich, Walter Hilton, Richard Rolle, Margery Kempe, and the author of *The Cloud of Unknowing,* all of whom wrote well before the sixteenth century. But one has to draw the line somewhere, and for reasons not entirely arbitrary this book cites only those who are heirs of the English Reformation.

The main purpose of this volume is not to introduce (or re-introduce) the reader to some great figures in the history of the church or to give her or him a taste of some fine prose, though clearly both of these things will be accomplished along the way. The primary justification for this collection is to enable some fairly authoritative voices from our own tradition to speak directly to us—to late-twentieth-century persons who are in need—heart to heart, mind to mind, soul to soul. We live in an era of pluralism and rapid social change; ours is a polytheistic age of shifting value centers and shaky commitments. Many times counselors even within the church neglect what Professor Don Browning of the University of Chicago has spoken of as "the moral context of pastoral care;" employing a method that is basically "eductive," they seek only to support the client as he or she "clarifies" his or her own values.[1] Of course, this therapeutic approach can be—has been—extremely helpful. To flee to the opposite extreme is to embrace legalism and moralism, and thus to risk the undermining of authentic selfhood. We are right to be wary of "the tyranny of the should" and to want to discover our own true path in life. But surely we have to acknowledge that the road we most often travel is not one that cuts through virgin forest but is rather a cluttered and often confusing route punctuated by signs and signals of every description. I think a person seeking trustworthy counsel is simply asking to be shown a few reliable signposts along the way.

In the Anglican tradition of spiritual reflection, there has always been a heavy emphasis placed upon personal

---

[1]Don S. Browning, *The Moral Context of Pastoral Care* (Philadelphia, 1976).

responsibility and the use of one's own (not unaided) powers of thinking and willing. As Stephen Neill has pointed out, "the Anglican appeal is to the intellect, the conscience, and the will." The individual who must decide and choose is not left alone, however, but is sustained by the Body of Christ.[2]

St. Augustine well understood the need that all Christians have of this continuing assistance. In his biography of the bishop of Hippo, Peter Brown notes that the *Confessions* did not give the conventional Christian of sixteen hundred years ago quite what he or she wanted: the book came as a surprise and an annoyance to many. Why? Because it was not the account of a successful conversion, not the story of a total transformation simple and dramatic and final. Augustine's experience of conversion did not mean that he had now arrived safely in port. Augustine makes it clear that the harbor of the convert was still buffeted by storms, or, in another image, that even the baptized Christian must remain an invalid.[3] Brown writes: "like the wounded man, found near death by the wayside in the Parable of the Good Samaritan, [Augustine's] life had been saved by the rite of baptism; but he must be content to endure, for the rest of his life, a prolonged and precarious convalescence in the 'Inn' of the Church."[4]

The authors of the passages quoted in this book may be thought of as experienced, well-recommended servants at this Inn. Some of the names will be familiar to readers. A large number of you will already have read *The Screwtape Letters*, by **C.S. Lewis** (1898-1963), who taught English literature for many years at Oxford and

---

[2]Stephen Neill, *Anglicanism* (Baltimore, 1965), pp. 423-424.

[3]Peter Brown, *Augustine of Hippo: A Biography* (Berkeley, Calif., 1967), pp. 177, 365.

[4]Brown, *Augustine*, p. 365.

Cambridge. For those who have not read this book, I need to point out that the letters are written by a senior devil in hell, Screwtape, to a junior tempter, Wormwood. It is Screwtape's custom to refer to Satan as "Our Father Below" and to God as "the Enemy." Before each of the excerpts from this book, I have inserted the phrase "Screwtape to Wormwood" to remind the reader of the shift in perspective.

Lewis' close friend **Austin Farrer** (1906-1968) is the source for the largest batch of quotations here. Farrer was an Anglican priest who spent most of his life teaching theology at Oxford, ending his days as warden of Keble College. Many regard him as the most impressive theologian the Church of England has produced in this century. Farrer dealt with the most difficult topics in philosophical theology (such as the problem of evil, in *Love Almighty and Ills Unlimited*), but he did so with a poet's imagination and in prose that is unusually well wrought.

Four other twentieth-century British clergymen are represented here.

William Temple (1882-1944) was archbishop of York from 1929 to 1942, when he became archbishop of Canterbury. He was a leader in the ecumenical movement and instrumental in the founding of the World Council of Churches. His most important work of theology is *Nature, Man and God* (1934).

After serving for nearly thirty years in parochial ministry, **Gordon Jeff** (b. 1932) is currently chaplain to St. Michael's Convent, Ham Common, in Richmond, Surrey. He is a founding member of SPIDIR, a network formed in 1978 to foster the ministry of spiritual direction.

Alec R. Vidler (b. 1899) was editor of the journal *Theology* for twenty-five years and has written many books in Christian theology and church history. He was canon of St. George's Chapel, Windsor, from 1948 to 1956, and dean of King's College, Cambridge, from 1956 to 1966. From 1972 to 1974 he served as mayor of Rye, England.

John Macquarrie (b. 1919) was educated at the University of Glasgow, where he taught before becoming professor of systematic theology at Union Theological Seminary in New York in 1962. From 1970 until his retirement in 1986, he held the Lady Margaret professorship of divinity in the University of Oxford. Strongly influenced by twentieth-century existentialist philosophy, Macquarrie has published numerous books in theology, ethics, and spirituality. His Gifford Lectures at the University of St. Andrews appeared in 1984 under the title *In Search of Deity*. His most recent book is *Jesus Christ in Modern Thought* (1990).

A devoted laywoman, **Dorothy Leigh Sayers** (1893-1957) wrote religious dramas, theological essays, and studies of Dante, but she is chiefly remembered today as the author of detective novels and short stories featuring Lord Peter Wimsey. Sayers completed her studies at Somerville College, Oxford, in 1915, taking first-class honors in medieval literature. She was one of the first women to receive a degree from that university.

An American layman, **Allan Mitchell Parrent** (b. 1930) received his doctorate in Christian ethics from Duke University. He is professor of ethics and associate dean for academic affairs at Virginia Theological Seminary, in Alexandria. He is a member of the Standing Commission on Peace of the Episcopal Church.

From the nineteenth century we have excerpts from a couple of letters by **E.B. Pusey** (1800-1882), Regius professor of Hebrew at Oxford for many decades and leader of the anglo-catholic revival movement known as tractarianism.

Although maintaining ecclesiastical balance was not part of any deliberate plan, we also have a representative of the evangelical wing of the church. **Hannah More**

9

(1745-1833) was active in the Sunday school movement; with her sister she started a chain of schools in the west of England where the poor were taught to read. She was also a popular religious writer. One of her best-known works, *Practical Piety*, is excerpted thrice below.

We are not entirely certain who wrote one of our sources, *The Whole Duty of Man*, the preeminent book of religious instruction of the eighteenth century. Its probable author is **Richard Allestree** (1619-1681), an Anglican priest who served from 1663 to 1679 as Regius professor of divinity at Oxford.

John Donne (1573-1631), author of the opening selection of this volume, spent his earlier years in recklessness and profligacy but eventually became not only a great poet but also a great preacher. He was ordained in 1615 and became dean of St. Paul's, London, in 1621.

Jeremy Taylor (1613-1667), author of *The Rule and Exercise of Holy Living* (1650), is representative of the strong practical emphasis in Anglicanism, stressing morality over dogma. Taylor was a fellow of All Souls College, Oxford, and, from 1660 to 1667, bishop of Down and Connor, in Ireland.

The nineteenth-century English critic and essayist Matthew Arnold wrote in *Culture and Anarchy* that Bishop Wilson's *Maxims* are not well known any more but "deserve to be [reprinted and] circulated as a religious book." He found "something peculiarly sincere and first-hand about them," admiring their "downright honesty and plain good sense."[5] **Thomas Wilson** (1663-1755) received an education in medical studies at Trinity College, Dublin, and became bishop of Sodor and Man in 1698, serving until the end of his long life.

William Law (1686-1761) is author of seven of our selections. His straightforward style, his insistence espe-

---

[5]Matthew Arnold, *Culture and Anarchy*, ed. J. Dover Wilson (Cambridge, Eng., 1960), pp. 4, 5.

cially on the virtues important in everyday life, and his own keen intellect and devout character have always won him many grateful readers, John Wesley and George Whitefield among them. Dr. Samuel Johnson said that *A Serious Call* (1728) was the book that first prompted him to think in earnest about the life of religion.[6] J.W.C. Wand, former bishop of London, has stated that this book "is perhaps the most eloquent and persuasive appeal for whole-hearted devotion that we have in the English language."[7] Born in King's Cliffe, Northamptonshire, Law was educated at Emmanuel College, Cambridge, and ordained in 1711. He lived in the household of Edward Gibbon, near London, from 1727 to 1737, serving as tutor to the father of the historian. Around 1740 he returned to his home in King's Cliffe and lived the remainder of his years in quiet retirement.

These, then, are our guides. I could not write a book of spiritual counsel myself, and I cannot tell you now precisely how to use this little collection. I have torn these passages from their original contexts, made up short titles for each of them, and placed them in some kind of order. So I have created enough of a disturbance as it is. Of course you would be right to suppose that I have found that many of these sentences have an extraordinary capacity to speak directly to my own condition, to my own broken self. But I cannot do more at this point than to say, now you have the words and the thoughts to address or not to address who you are, where you are.

David Hein
February 21, 1991
Frederick, Maryland

---

[6]W. Jackson Bate, *Samuel Johnson* (New York, 1979), p. 102.

[7]J.W.C. Wand, *Anglicanism in History and Today* (London, 1961), p. 80.

11

—BEGINNING: PRAYER—

Seasons for Prayer

God hath made no decree to distinguish the seasons of his mercies; in paradise, the fruits were ripe the first minute, and in heaven it is always autumn, his mercies are ever in their maturity. We ask *panem quotidianum*, our daily bread, and God never says you should have come yesterday, he never says, you must again tomorrow, but *today if you will hear his voice*, today he will hear you. If some king of the earth have so large an extent of dominion, in north and south, as that he hath winter and summer together in his dominions, much more hath God mercy and judgement together: he brought light out of darkness, not out of a lesser light; he can bring thy summer out of winter, though thou have no spring; though in the ways of fortune, or understanding, or conscience, thou have been benighted till now, wintered and frozen, clouded and eclipsed, damped and benumbed, smothered and stupified till now, now God comes to thee, not as in the dawning of the day, not as in the bud of the spring, but as the sun at noon to illustrate all shadows, as the sheaves in harvest, to fill all penuries. All occasions invite his mercies, and all times are his seasons.

Donne, *Sermons*, vol. 2, p. 172.

How Shall I Live?

We must pray, for prayer is neither more nor less than living with God. Shall I live today of myself and by myself, or shall I live it with God? Doubtless, whether or not I live it with God, God lives it with me—but that only makes it the more monstrous that I should not live it with him. Prayer is just living with God: looking at him, regarding his will, reaching out our hands for the blessings he is so eager to give, bringing our action into his. We must pray. If you cannot pray, come and ask for help. What could be more natural, than for a Christian to say to a priest, may I make a date to talk to you about my prayers? What else are we for?

Farrer, *The End of Man*, p. 106.

Petitioning God

We are to petition also for our Bodies; that is, we are to ask of God such necessaries of life as are needful to use, while we live here. But these only in such a degree and measure, as his wisdom sees best for us: we must not presume to be our own Carvers, and pray for all that wealth or greatness, which our vain hearts may perhaps desire, but only for such a condition in respect of outward things, as he sees may most tend to those great ends of our living here, the glorifying [of] him, and the saving of our own souls.

Allestree, *The Whole Duty of Man*, p. 104.

Praying and Loving

There is nothing that makes us love a man so much as praying for him; and when you can once do this sincerely for any man, you have fitted your soul for the performance of everything that is kind and civil toward him. This will fill your heart with a generosity and tenderness that will give you a better and sweeter behavior than anything that is called fine breeding and good manners.

By considering yourself as an advocate with God for

14

your neighbors and acquaintances, you would never find it hard to be at peace with them yourself. It would be easy to you to bear with and forgive those for whom you particularly implored the divine mercy and forgiveness.

Law, *A Serious Call*, p. 302.

When We Say the Lord's Prayer

Notice that we are taught to pray not: 'Give me my daily bread,' but 'Give us our daily bread.' We pray to the Father of all for the whole human family. That is why, if we are going to be literal-minded, it makes good sense for us, last thing at night, to pray 'Give us this day our daily bread.' For when we are going to bed, the sun is rising and a new day is beginning in other countries and in other parts of the world. When we say the Lord's Prayer, we are praying for them as well as for ourselves.

Of course, we could not pray with integrity that all our fellow human beings may have their daily bread, if we were not prepared to do everything in our power to see that they do have it . . .

Vidler, *Windsor Sermons*, p. 116.

Confessing the Truth about Ourselves

When Thomas said to his fellow-disciples, 'unless I see and touch, I shall not believe', what do you think it was? Was it a refusal, or a boast, or a confession? A refusal—I won't believe: or a boast—I'm too clever to believe: or a confession—I shan't be able to believe? He was a friend and disciple of Christ's, who had risked his life with him: how could he refuse to believe that God had raised him from the dead? or how boast of sceptical detachment, who had committed himself to a cause, body and soul? No, surely it was more like a confession: That's

15

the sort of man I am; I shan't be able to believe, unless I believe my own hands, and eyes. If, when he said this, Thomas was telling the truth, he could hardly have done better: do you think he would have done better if he had lied? If he had pretended to believe, when he didn't? When we come to Christ in our prayer, shall we tell him a pack of lies? Shall we pretend all sorts of noble sentiments we do not have: pretend to believe in him as firmly as we believe our own existence, pretend to care for his holy will as warmly and constantly as we care for our own comforts and ambitions? Of course not; for whom could we hope to deceive? Not him: we could only deceive ourselves. No, we will confess ourselves as we are, and know that he will treat us on our level, and according to our need, as he did Thomas: reach hither thy finger, and feel my hands; reach hither thy hand, and put it in my side; go not in lack of faith but believe.

Farrer, *A Celebration of Faith*, p. 79.

—SUBMISSION TO GOD—

Thy will be done

There is a haughty spirit which though it will not complain, does not care to submit. It arrogates to itself the dignity of enduring, without any claim to the meekness of yielding. Its silence is stubbornness, its fortitude is pride; its calmness is apathy without, and discontent within. In such characters, it is not so much the will of God which is the rule of conduct, as the scorn of pusillanimity. Not seldom indeed the mind puts in a claim for a merit to which the nerves could make out a better title . . . True resignation is the hardest lesson in the whole school of Christ. It is the oftenest taught and the latest learnt. It is not a task which, when once got over in some particular instance, leaves us master of the subject. The necessity of following up the lesson we have begun, presents itself almost every day in some new shape . . . The submission of yesterday does not exonerate us from the resignation of to-day. The principle, indeed, once thoroughly wrought into the soul, gradually reconciles to the frequent demand for its exercise, and renders every successive call more easily.

Submission is a duty of such high and holy import that it can only be learnt of the Great Teacher. If it could have been acquired by mere moral institution, the wise sayings of the ancient philosophers would have taught it . . .

We must remember, that in offering this prayer ["Thy will be done"], we may by our own request, be offering to resign what we most dread to lose, to give up what is dear to us as our own soul; we may be recalling our own Heavenly Father to withhold what we are most anxiously labouring to obtain, and to withdraw what we are most sedulously endeavouring to keep. We are most solemnly renouncing our property in ourselves, we are distinctly making ourselves over again to Him whose we already are. We specifically entreat him to do with us what he pleases, to mould us to a conformity to his image, without which we shall never be resigned to his will. In short, to dispose of us as his infinite wisdom sees best, however contrary to the scheme which our blindness has laid down as the path to unquestionable happiness.

To render this trying petition easy to us, is one great reason why God by such a variety of providences, afflicts and brings us low.

He knows we want incentives to humility, even more than incitements to virtuous actions. He shows us in many ways, that self-sufficiency and happiness are incompatible, that pride and peace are irreconcilable; that, following our own way, and doing our own will, which we consider to be the very essence of felicity, is in direct opposition to it.

More, *Christian Morals*, pp. 131-132.

Real Resignation

Screwtape to Wormwood:

What the Enemy means by this [submission to His will] is primarily that [the patient] should accept . . . the tribulation which has actually been dealt out to him—the present anxiety and suspense. It is about *this* that he is to say "Thy will be done," and for the daily task of bearing *this* that the daily bread will be provided. It is your business to see that the patient never thinks of the present fear as his appointed cross, but only of the things he is afraid of. Let him regard them as his crosses: let him forget that, since they are incompatible, they cannot all happen to him, and let him try to practise fortitude and patience to them all in advance. For real resignation, at the same moment, to a dozen different and hypothetical fates, is almost impossible, and the Enemy does not greatly assist those who are trying to attain it: resignation to present and actual suffering, even where that suffering consists of fear, is far easier, and is usually helped by this direct action.

Lewis, *The Screwtape Letters*, p. 29.

Trust in God

Shall we reduce St. Mark's Gospel to three lines?

God gives you everything.
Give everything to God.
You can't.

True, there is a fourth line; Christ will make you able, for he has risen from the dead. But this is almost over-shadowed in St. Mark's Gospel by the emphasis on self-distrust. St. Mark seems even more afraid that his readers will trust themselves than that they will distrust Christ's risen power.

Perhaps the Mark of the gospel was the John Mark of Acts after all. And perhaps all this emphasis on deser-tion, running away, the failure of good intentions has something to do with that most painful text in the Book of Acts: "Barnabas wished to take John called Mark with them; but Paul thought it not well to take with them him who had turned back from them in Pamphylia, and not gone with them to the work." If the Evangelist is that Mark who had once turned back, and of whom St. Paul had thought the worse for his turning back, then he had evidently learned from his turning back what God wished him to learn from it: that it is not in us to follow Christ, it is Christ's gift.

Happy is the man who learns from his own failures. He certainly won't learn from anyone else's. Here I am on safe ground, for when it comes to serving God we are all failures, are we not? So there is no fear of my missing my target in any of my readers. It is humiliating how, especially in the bosom of our families, childish faults of temper reassert themselves which we hoped we had outgrown; humiliating how, as soon as a change of scene removes the encouraging company of our Christian friends, our religion languishes. We have not prayed nor worked nor controlled ourselves as we hoped to do. God has given us much; we have not given anything worth mentioning to God. Well, St. Mark (if he is indeed the same man) went back from the work in Pamphylia, and in Gethsemane none of the disciples behaved with credit.

It is by these desolating experiences that God teaches us to trust him, not ourselves. The more emptied out we are, the more hope there is of our learning to be Christians. Now is the very moment—there will never be a better—for us to put our trust in the God who makes something from nothing, who raises the dead.

Farrer, *A Faith of Our Own*, pp. 112-114.

Invoking the Holy Spirit

When we pray 'Come, Holy Ghost, our souls inspire', we had better know what we are about. He will not carry us to easy triumphs and gratifying successes; more probably he will set us to some task for God in the full intention that we shall fail, so that others, learning wisdom by our failure, may carry the good cause forward. He may take us through loneliness, desertion by friends, apparent desertion even by God; that was the way Christ went to the Father. He may drive us into the wilderness to be tempted of the devil. He may lead us from the Mount of Transfiguration (if he ever lets us climb it) to the hill that is called the Place of a Skull. For if we invoke him, it must be to help us in doing God's will, not ours. We cannot call upon the

> *Creator Spirit, by whose aid*
> *The world's foundations first were laid*

in order to use omnipotence for the supply of our futile pleasures or the success of our futile plans. If we invoke him, we must be ready for the glorious pain of being caught by his power out of our petty orbit into the eternal purposes of the Almighty, in whose onward sweep our lives are as a speck of dust. The soul that is filled with the Spirit must have become purged of all pride or love of ease, all self-complacence and self-reliance; but that soul has found the only real dignity, the only lasting joy. Come then, Great Spirit, come. Convict the world; and convict my timid soul.

Temple, *Readings*, pp. 288-289.

Nonetheless

Screwtape to Wormwood:

Our cause is never more in danger than when a human, no longer desiring, but still intending, to do our Enemy's will, looks round upon a universe from which every trace of Him seems to have vanished, and asks why he has been forsaken, and still obeys.

Lewis, *The Screwtape Letters*, p. 39.

—— HUMILITY ——

Pride and Piety

No people have more occasion to be afraid of the approaches of pride than those who have made some advances in a pious life. For pride can grow as well upon our virtues as upon our vices, and steals upon us on all occasions.

Every good thought that we have, every good action that we do, lays us open to pride and exposes us to the assaults of vanity and self-satisfaction.

Law, *A Serious Call*, pp. 228-229.

Reason and Pride

God Almighty has entrusted us with the use of reason, and we use it to the disorder and corruption of our nature. We reason ourselves into all kinds of folly and misery, and make our lives the sport of foolish and extravagant passions, seeking after imaginary happiness in all kinds of shapes, creating to ourselves a thousand wants, amusing our hearts with false hopes and fears, using the world worse than irrational animals, envying, vexing, and tormenting one another with restless passions and unreasonable contentions.

Let any man but look back upon his own life and see what use he has made of his reason, how little he has consulted it, and how less he has followed it. What foolish passions, what vain thoughts, what needless labors, what extravagant projects, have taken up the greatest part of his life. How foolish he has been in his words and conversation, how seldom he has done well with judgment, and how often he has been kept from doing ill by accident; how seldom he has been able to please himself, and how often he has displeased others; how often he has changed his counsels, hated what he loved and loved what he hated; how often he has been enraged and transported at trifles, pleased and displeased with the very same things, and constantly changing from one vanity to another. Let a man but take this view of his own life, and he will see reason enough to confess that pride was not made for man.

Law, *A Serious Call*, p. 230.

Self-Regard

Screwtape to Wormwood:

By this method thousands of humans have been brought to think that humility means pretty women trying to believe they are ugly and clever men trying to believe they are fools. And since what they are trying to believe may, in some cases, be manifest nonsense, they cannot succeed in believing it, and we have the chance of keeping their minds endlessly revolving on themselves in an effort to achieve the impossible. To anticipate the Enemy's strategy, we must consider His aims. The Enemy wants to bring the man to a state of mind in which he could design the best cathedral in the world, and know it to be the best, and rejoice in the fact, without being any more (or less) or otherwise glad at having done it than he would be if it had been done by another. The Enemy wants him, in the end, to be so free from any bias in his own favour that he can rejoice in his own talents as frankly and gratefully as in his neighbour's talents—or in a sunrise, an elephant, or a waterfall. He wants each man, in the long run, to be able to recognise all creatures (even himself) as glorious and excellent things. He wants to kill their animal self-love as soon as possible; but it is His long-term policy, I fear, to restore to them a new kind of self-love—a charity and gratitude for all selves, including their own; when they have really learned to love their neighbours as themselves, they will be allowed to love themselves as their neighbours.

Lewis, *The Screwtape Letters*, pp. 64-65.

——— MY OWN CALLING ———

Be Not Ashamed . . .

Never be ashamed of thy birth, or thy parents, or thy trade, or thy present imployment, for the meannesse or poverty of any of them: and when there is an occasion to speak of them, such an occasion as would invite you to speak of any thing that pleases you, omit it not; but speak as readily and indifferently of thy meannesse, as of thy greatnesse. *Primislaus* the first King of *Bohemia* kept his countrey shooes alwayes by him, to remember from whence he was raised: and *Agathocles* by the furniture of his Table confessed, that from a Potter he was raised to be the King of *Sicily*.

Taylor, *Holy Living*, p. 90.

The Quest of the Self

It is easy to say, 'Be yourself', if you could find the self you are supposed to be: but what is it? Some people think that they are being themselves, and wonderfully sincere, if they identify themselves with their worst and most primitive passions. But that is to be little better than an animal, and how can I be myself by being a beast? I am a man, surely, and how can I be myself by forgetting my noblest part? Where is the sincerity in a man's being a beast? Yet if I attempt to follow a higher ideal of myself, how easily do I become a prig or a hypocrite.

The saint has solved the problem of sincerity in the sole possible way by turning to God, the great I AM, and accepting the self his creator designed for him. And the quest of the self God has meant each of us to be is like the quest of happiness (which is indeed much the same

27

thing)—it is not found by looking for it. We do not ask of God, 'What sort of person did you mean me to be?'—we say to him 'Lord, what wilt thou have me to do?'

Farrer, *A Celebration of Faith*, pp. 199-200.

Vocation

The one question is, whether God calls us: it is not whether we feel fit or no. If God gives us the call, God will give us the grace. We may under-estimate ourselves, as well as over-estimate ourselves. St. Paul said, "Who is sufficient for these things?" If St. Paul, how much more we? The question is not as to anything in the past or present; but as to the call of God. If God calls us, He will fit us. When God put our soul into the bodies which we received of our parents, He had His own special purpose for each of us. He willed each of us to be saved in doing our own appointed work. He had us and our whole selves to be formed in our own special way. We sometimes hear of a person mistaking his profession; of his being, e.g., a good lawyer spoiled, a good man of business spoiled, i.e. he had missed the employment of life for which God adapted [him].

I cannot tell what your calling is: I know only certain outward dispositions: hold up your soul as a sheet of white paper to God, for Him to write on it what He wills. He has promised to hear prayer: say with St. Augustine, "Give what Thou commandest, and command what Thou willest." Do not hurry, but pray Him to teach you.

Pusey, *Spiritual Letters*, p. 23.

Work

Don't be too easily convinced that God really wants you to do all sorts of work you needn't do. Each must do his duty "in that state of life to which God has called him."

. . . there can be intemperance in work just as in drink. What feels like zeal may be only fidgets or even the flattering of one's self-importance. As MacDonald says "In holy things may be unholy greed." And by doing what "one's station and its duties" does not demand, one can make oneself less fit for the duties it does demand and so commit some injustice. Just you give Mary a little chance as well as Martha!

Lewis, *Letters to an American Lady*, pp. 50-51.

—VICE AND VIRTUE
IN DAILY LIFE—

The Hourly Occasions

Vanity is at the bottom of almost all, may we not say, of all our sins? We think more of signalizing than of saving ourselves. We overlook the hourly occasions which occur of serving, of obliging, of comforting those around us, while we sometimes, not unwillingly perform an act of notorious generosity. The habit however in the former case better indicates the disposition and bent of the mind, than the solitary act of splendour. The Apostle does not say whatsoever *great* things ye do, but "whatsoever things ye do, do *all* to the glory of God."

More, *Practical Piety*, p. 132.

Ordinary Actions and Occasional Prayers

As sure therefore as there is any wisdom in praying for the Spirit of God, so sure is it that we are to make that Spirit the rule of all our actions; as sure as it is our duty to look wholly unto God in our prayers, so sure is it that it is our duty to live wholly unto God in our lives. But we can no more be said to live unto God unless we live unto Him in all the ordinary actions of our life, unless He be the rule and measure of all our ways, than we can be said to pray unto God unless our prayer look wholly unto Him. So that unreasonable and absurd ways of life, whether in labor or diversion, whether they consume our time or our money, are like unreasonable and absurd prayers and are as truly an offence unto God.

. . . You see [many people] strict as to some times and places of devotion, but when the service of the church is over, they are but like those that seldom or never come there. In their way of life, their manner of spending their time and money, in their cares and fears, in their pleasures and indulgences, in their labor and diversions, they are like the rest of the world. This makes the loose part of the world generally make a jest of those that are devout because they see their devotion goes no further than their prayers, and that when they are over they live no more unto God till the time of prayer returns again, but live by the same humour and fancy and in as full an enjoyment of all the follies of life as other people. This is the reason why they are the jest and scorn of careless and worldly people, not because they are really devoted to God, but because they appear to have no other devotion but that of occasional prayers.

Law, *A Serious Call*, p. 48.

Self-Awareness

Screwtape to Wormwood:

One can therefore formulate the general rule: In all activities of mind which favour our cause, encourage the patient to be un-selfconscious and to concentrate on the object, but in all activities favourable to the Enemy bend his mind back on itself. Let an insult or a woman's body so fix his attention outward that he does not reflect "I am now entering into the state called Anger—or the state called Lust." Contrariwise let the reflection "My feelings are now growing more devout, or more charitable," so fix his attentions inward that he no longer looks beyond himself to see our Enemy or his own neighbours.

Lewis, *The Screwtape Letters*, pp. 29-30.

Virtue and Vice

We should cultivate most assiduously, because the work is so difficult, those graces which are most opposite to our natural temper; the value of our good qualities depending much on their being produced by the victory over some natural wrong propensity. The implantation of a virtue is the eradication of a vice. It will cost one man more to keep down a rising passion than to do a brilliant deed. It will try another more to keep back a sparkling but corrupt thought, which his wit had suggested but which his religion checks, than it would to give a large sum in charity.

More, *Practical Piety*, p. 30.

Cleverness

Cleverness is a great temptation to vanity. The single remarks strike persons, and they admire them. Some smile shows it; and the person goes his way and is self-satisfied and his vanity is nourished . . .

Now just watch yourself for the little occasions in which you think yourself cleverer than another. Perhaps you won't call it clever, but something more solid; a true perception of things. Set yourself against any supposed superiority to any one. One grain of love is better than a hundredweight of intellect. And after all, that blasted spirit, Satan, has more intellect than the whole human race.

Pusey, *Spiritual Letters*, p. 105.

Lust and Disillusionment

About the sin called *Luxuria* or *Lust*, I shall . . . say only three things. First, that it is a sin, and that it ought to be called plainly by its own name, and neither huddled away under a generic term like immorality, nor confused with love.

Secondly, that up till now the Church, in hunting down this sin, has had the active alliance of Caesar, who has been concerned to maintain family solidarity and the orderly devolution of property in the interests of the State. But now that contract and not status is held to be the basis of society, Caesar need no longer rely on the family to maintain social solidarity; and now that so much property is held anonymously by trusts and joint-stock companies, the laws of inheritance lose a great deal of their importance. Consequently, Caesar is now much less interested than he was in the sleeping arrangements of his citizens, and has in this matter cynically denounced his alliance with the Church. This is a warning against putting one's trust in any child of man—particularly in Caesar. If the Church is to continue her campaign against Lust, she must do so on her own—that is, on sacramental—grounds; and she will have to do it, if not in defiance of Caesar, at least without his assistance.

Thirdly, there are two main reasons for which people fall into the sin of Luxuria. It may be through sheer exuberance of animal spirits: in which case a sharp application of the curb may be all that is needed to bring the body into subjection and remind it of its proper place in the scheme of man's twofold nature. Or—and this commonly happens in periods of disillusionment like our own, when philosophies are bankrupt and life appears without hope—men and women may turn to lust in sheer boredom and discontent, trying to find in it some stimulus which is not provided by the drab discomfort of their mental and physical surroundings. When *that* is the case, stern rebukes and restrictions are worse than useless. It is as though one were to endeavour to cure anaemia by bleeding; it only reduces further an already impoverished vitality. The mournful and medical aspect of twentieth-century pornography and promiscuity strongly suggests that we have reached one of these periods of spiritual depression, where people go to bed because they have nothing better to do. In other words, the "regrettable moral laxity" of which respectable people complain may have its root cause not in Luxuria at all, but in some other of the sins of society, and may automatically begin to cure itself when that root cause is removed.

Sayers, *Creed or Chaos?*, pp. 63-64.

The Desires that Disturb Human Life

The man of pride has a thousand wants which only his own pride has created, and these render him as full of trouble as if God had created him with a thousand appetites without creating anything that was proper to satisfy them. Envy and ambition have also their endless wants which disquiet the souls of men, and by their contradictory motions render them as foolishly miserable as those that want to fly and creep at the same time . . .

For all the wants which disturb human life, which make us uneasy to ourselves, quarrelsome with others, and unthankful to God, which weary us in vain labors and foolish anxieties, which carry us from project to project, from place to place in a poor pursuit of we don't know what, are the wants which neither God, nor nature, nor reason hath subjected us to, but are solely infused into us by pride, envy, ambition, and covetousness.

Law, *A Serious Call*, pp. 150, 153.

Christian Realism

There is a "Masterpiece Theatre" production entitled "Paradise Postponed," a poignant story of an Anglican cleric who, in the words of that lovely English hymn, sought to "build Jerusalem in England's green and pleasant land." After his death one of his sons, lamenting his late father's idealistic beliefs, says:

The trouble with our father's paradise is that it keeps getting put off, doesn't it? The promised land is always just around the corner. All we seem to get is paradise postponed.

The son's analysis rings true to all of us who have had our particular paradises postponed. But that analysis is also dangerous. It is dangerous because it can lead to despair on the one hand or to fanaticism on the other. It can lead to a total resignation to what is a despairing attitude of "what's the use?" Or it can lead to a total fanatical commitment to forcing a reluctant humankind around that last corner to paradise, whatever the human cost. . .

But the Gospel offers us a way through these twin dangers. Despair is the fate of those who know something about sin but nothing about redemption. Fanaticism is the fate of those who know something about redemption but not enough about sin. Through the life, death, and resurrection of Christ we as Christians know something about both. In the Eucharist we acknowledge both, confessing our sin and giving thanks for our redemption. We declare our anticipation of the promised Resurrection and express our thanks that we have been made heirs, through hope, of God's eternal kingdom.

It is the hope in the Resurrection that frees us to involve ourselves in the necessary but always imperfect structures that order our common life in this age. It is the assurance that at the last day God will bring us into the joy of his eternal kingdom that frees us to work toward a just and humane society in this age, and to do so without succumbing to despair over a paradise postponed or to

36

fanaticism for an imagined paradise just around the corner.

Parrent, "This Age and That Age," *Best Sermons 1*, pp. 214-215.

Acquaintance with Misery

An overmastering sense of human ills can be taken as the world's invitation to deny her Maker, or it may be taken as God's invitation to succor his world. Which is it to be? Those who take the practical alternative become more closely and more widely acquainted with misery than the onlookers; but they feel the grain of existence, and the movement of the purposes of God. They do not argue, they love; and what is loved is always known as good. The more we love, the more we feel the evils besetting or corrupting the object of our love. But the more we feel the force of the besetting harms, the more certain we are of the value residing in what they attack; and in resisting them are identified with the action of God, whose mercy is over all flesh.

Farrer, *Love Almighty*, pp. 164-165.

Christian Living

A christian lives at the height of his being, not only at the top of his spiritual, but of his intellectual life. He alone lives in the full exercise of his rational powers. Religion ennobles his reason while it enlarges it.

Let, then, your soul act up to its high destination; let not that which was made to soar to heaven, grovel in the dust. Let it not live so much below itself. You wonder it is not more fixed, when it is perpetually resting on things which are not fixed themselves. In the rest of a christian there is a stability. Nothing can shake his confidence but sin. Outward attacks and troubles rather fix than unsettle him, as tempests from without only serve to root the oak faster, while an inward canker will gradually rot and decay it.

More, *Practical Piety*, p. 48.

Enjoying Creation

Screwtape to Wormwood:

I would make it a rule to eradicate from my patient any strong personal taste which is not actually a sin, even if it is something quite trivial such as a fondness for county cricket or collecting stamps or drinking cocoa. Such things, I grant you, have nothing of virtue in them; but there is a sort of innocence and humility and self-forget-fulness about them which I distrust. The man who truly and disinterestedly enjoys any one thing in the world, for its own sake, and without caring twopence what other people say about it, is by that very fact forearmed against some of our subtlest modes of attack.

Lewis, *The Screwtape Letters*, p. 60.

—HUMAN BEINGS
AND NATURE —

God the Author of Nature

I worship the God of beauty. Human skill, I tell myself, is proud to have arranged a single pattern of aesthetic charm on a few feet of painted canvas; divine contrivance has set a whole landscape in everlasting rock, in rushing torrents and in springing trees. And in telling myself this I do not err. That adaptation of my eye to environment, and of environment to my eye, which produces aesthetic delight, is a masterpiece of God's skill. Not only has he created man, he has fitted him to his environment in a hundred subtle ways; among which not the least remarkable is this relation of things to our eye, giving aesthetic delight, and sometimes ecstasy.

Only I must beware of over-humanising, or of taking the comparison between God and the painter too far. The painter thinks of nothing but the picture. He is interested in the paint and canvas solely for the way they can be made to look. What their chemical composition may be, what active processes are going on in the atoms that make them up, is of no concern to him. He is merely careful to select materials which will place no obstacles in his way, nor do anything to cramp his liberty in painting. If then I allow myself to think of God as an artist in living landscape, I shall wonder why he uses materials which are so largely irrelevant to his purpose, so frustrating; and I shall notice that, while some of his works are supremely beautiful, some are humdrum to the eye, some hideous and discordant; as though his materials had got out of hand and defeated his artistry.

What is my mistake? I have forgotten that God is the

Cause of the world's existence, and that he has woven nature up from the bottom. That natural beauty which is such a charm in my eyes is, as it were, a divine after-thought; a sweet enjoyment for mankind in the look of a world whose existence serves quite other ends. Scenic beauty belongs to the sphere of man, and man was a late arrival. The masses of the mountains were not trimmed for human eyes; landscape is not a landscape-garden. God's goodness is not disappointed because not all scenes are equally lovely to us. God does not form ideal projects and regret to find them imperfectly realizable. He rejoices that rocks and trees, rivers and meadows, created on quite other principles, afford such feasts to human eyes.

Farrer, *God Is Not Dead*, pp. 72-74.

Animals

Listen to the poets of Israel: 'Oh God, thou preservest man and beast.' 'The eyes of all wait upon thee.' 'He causeth grass to grow for the cattle.' 'The high hills are a refuge for the wild goats, and the rocks for the conies.' And then there is that superb outburst of music which closes the whole psalter and calls upon 'everything that hath breath' to 'praise the Lord'. Among the prophets of Israel we note that Isaiah bids his people learn lessons from the ox and the ass. Balaam is rebuked for striking the animal on which he rode. Jonah is reproved for his inhumanity in failing to consider not only the children but the cattle which would be included in the judgment that he invoked on the city of Nineveh. So our Lord Jesus Christ was fulfilling the best traditions of his people when he showed his sympathy with the foxes who had holes and the birds that had nests, and when he said that, though five sparrows were sold for a farthing, not one of them fell to the ground without the Father's knowledge.

He compared, you remember, his own love for the people of Jerusalem with that of a mother hen gathering her chickens under her wings . . .

[People] can be sentimental and silly about animals, but it is a fact that we are bound up with the animals in God's creation. We depend on them and they depend on us. They are at our mercy . . . The very power we have over them entitles them to our care and protection as children are entitled to the care and protection of their parents. As Browning said:

God made all creatures and gave them our love and our fear, To give sign, we and they are his children, one family here . . .

Care and compassion for animals has a way of clearing the channels of communication with God.

He prayeth best who loveth best
All creatures great and small.

'Blessed are the merciful, for they shall obtain mercy.' Many good men have indeed had their thoughts turned and raised to God by contemplating the animals and in consequence have taken part with more fervour in the worship of God. John Keble wrote a poem 'To a thrush singing in January':

Sweet bird, up earliest in the morn,
Up earliest in the year,
Far in the quiet mist are borne
Thy matins soft and clear.

For these and all his mercies God's holy name be praised.

Vidler, *Windsor Sermons*, pp. 174, 175, 176.

Loving the Created Order

I will never laugh at anyone for grieving over a loved beast. I think God wants us to love Him more, not to love creatures (even animals) less. We love everything in one way too much (i.e. at the expense of our love for Him) but in another way we love everything too little.

No person, animal, flower, or even pebble, has ever been loved too much—i.e. more than every one of God's works deserves.

Lewis, *Letters to an American Lady*, p. 58.

—— *FRIENDSHIP* ——

Friendship and Heaven

Those who cannot conceive Friendship as a substantive love but only as a disguise or elaboration of Eros betray the fact that they have never had a Friend. The rest of us know that though we can have erotic love and friendship for the same person yet in some ways nothing is less like a Friendship than a love-affair. Lovers are always talking to one another about their love; Friends hardly ever about their Friendship. Lovers are normally face to face, absorbed in each other; Friends, side by side, absorbed in some common interest. Above all, Eros (while it lasts) is necessarily between two only. But two, far from being the necessary number for Friendship, is not even the best. And the reason for this is important . . .

In each of my friends there is something that only some other friend can fully bring out. By myself I am not large enough to call the whole man into activity; I want other lights than my own to show all his facets. Now that Charles is dead, I shall never again see Ronald's reaction to a specifically Caroline joke. Far from having more of Ronald, having him "to myself" now that Charles is away, I have less of Ronald. Hence true Friendship is the least jealous of loves. Two friends delight to be joined by a third, and three by a fourth, if only the newcomer is qualified to become a real friend. They can then say, as the blessed souls say in Dante, "Here comes one who will augment our loves." For in this love "to divide is not to take away."

. . . In this, Friendship exhibits a glorious "nearness by resemblance" to Heaven itself where the very multitude of the blessed (which no man can number) increases the fruition which each has of God. For every soul, seeing

Him in her own way, doubtless communicates that unique vision to all the rest. That, says an old author, is why the Seraphim in Isaiah's vision are crying "Holy, Holy, Holy" *to one another* (Isaiah VI, 3). The more we thus share the Heavenly Bread between us, the more we shall all have.

Lewis, *The Four Loves*, pp. 91-93.

Friendship and Pride

The danger of . . . pride is . . . almost inseparable from Friendly love.   Friendship must exclude.   From the innocent and necessary act of excluding to the spirit of exclusiveness is an easy step; and thence to the degrading pleasure of exclusiveness. If that is once admitted the downward slope will grow rapidly steeper . . .

The common vision which first brought us together may fade quite away. We shall be a *coterie* that exists for the sake of being a *coterie*; a little self-elected (and therefore absurd) aristocracy, basking in the moonshine of our collective self-approval . . .

The mass of the people, who are never quite right, are never quite wrong. They are hopelessly mistaken in their belief that every knot of friends came into existence for the sake of the pleasures of conceit and superiority. They are, I trust, mistaken in their belief that every Friendship actually indulges in these pleasures. But they would seem to be right in diagnosing pride as the danger to which Friendships are naturally liable. Just because this is the most spiritual of loves the danger which besets it is spiritual too. Friendship is even, if you like, angelic. But man needs to be triply protected by humility if he is to eat the bread of angels without risk.

Lewis, *The Four Loves*, pp. 122, 123-124.

In Circles

The occasions for kindness ring us round in two circles. The inner circle is made up of our ordinary environment. How do you view the people among whom you move? Are you going to cultivate the successful and neglect the less attractive . . .? Are you ever going to ask, who needs friendship most? Of course there is a special place for our most congenial friends; it is another thing, if we shutter our minds against others, or close our doors.

So much for the inner circle of kindness, which touches us all the time; so surely it concerns us most. But then there is the outer circle, most distant, hungry and dark—the needs of those less privileged than we are.

Farrer, *The Brink of Mystery*, p. 55.

—MARRIAGE AND FAMILY—

An Entire Union

So many miserable reasons have been found for our behaving ourselves, and by contrast the biblical reason is so splendid. When St. Paul was writing to his still half-heathen Corinthians, all the reasons which have been current in worldly minds from then till now had already been found. The philosophers were saying, Passion is base, starve it; reason is noble, foster it; but the Bible has nothing to do with this sort of cultural snobbery. Lawyers were laying it down that wives are property not to be purloined, and marriageable girls marketable commodities not to be spoiled. Moses may speak in this strain, but Christ does not. Social utilitarians were pointing out how undesirable it is for fatherless children to get loose in the world. But the Bible never refers to this unquestionable nuisance as a reason to be chaste. No, the faith of Christ takes its stand on the integrity of the human person. We are to move in one piece, body, heart, and spirit, and not to commit our body to another until we commit our heart and soul in an entire and permanent union.

Farrer, *A Faith of Our Own*, pp. 208-209.

Marriage and the Wider World

In taking marriage into its sacramental structure, the Church breaks down the barrier between the sacred and the secular, declares its concern with our worldly, embodied existence, and provides for the impact of the divine grace upon our everyday activities. At first sight, it may seem strange that matrimony is reckoned a sacrament at all. Yet the recognition of its sacramental character forms an indispensable link between worship and life, and Christian marriage becomes the gateway through which the grace of holy Being made present in the sacraments can penetrate the wider world of human relationships . .

If prayer, worship, and the sacraments form the center of Christian life, then it must be said that the first concentric ring as one moves out from the center is the area of sex, marriage, and family life. The church has rightly seen that this area provides a bridgehead into the world, and that if these most intimate communal relations can be "sanctified," that is to say, made whole and healthy, then a decisive step has been taken toward eventually sanctifying the larger social relations that lie beyond.

Actually, it is not hard to see the immediate outreach of the sacramental idea beyond marriage and the family. The Christian doctrines of creation and incarnation, by recognizing the divine presence in the world and our own responsibility to cooperate with this presence in its work of creation-reconciliation-consummation, enable us to see the world and our policies of action in it with a new clarity and seriousness. The other person is seen as the neighbor, destined to have his place in the family of God. Even material things are to be seen in the light of Being and of our own status as stewards or shepherds or guardians of Being.

Macquarrie, *Principles*, pp. 513, 515.

Fathers

By sitting late over Greek print in a badly lighted library, I finished my eyes and Schools together. I was forbidden to read for three months. Not read for three months? What was I to do? 'Look,' said my father, 'the fence round the garden is falling to pieces, we'll replace it. We'll do it in oak; and we won't buy the uprights ready slotted, we'll cut them out with hand tools.' So we made that solid oak paling right round the garden, my father and I. I wonder whether it still stands? The weeks flew by, the long sunshiny days of satisfying manual labour. I never had a happier summer than that summer I was supposed to be blind. There was the pleasure of doing a great work, and overcoming hourly difficulties. But above all, there was the pleasure of working with my father, who did not make himself the boss—he accepted me as an equal. All the time there was the feeling of his kindness, who had undertaken such a labour to keep me cheerful; but there was nothing indebting in it, it was so obvious he enjoyed the work as much as I did. My zest, however great, could not equal his . . .

I know that it is all very well for me to go on like this, but that there may be no answering recollection in my audience—some of you don't have much to do with your fathers, and some of you wish you had less to do with them than you have . . .

I do hope that those of you who are having a sticky passage with your fathers, and have not got over the very necessary but painful business of achieving independence from paternal tyranny, will do all you can to re-establish relations on a basis of equality as soon as possible. Do it, while the going is good: you will not have your fathers always. When my present College was so kind as to suggest my coming into it, how I should have liked to talk to my father about it, but alas!

Do you ever write to your fathers? It is an amiable and can even be an enjoyable exercise. There is a special reason. God has made known to us the mysteries of his kindness through human parables. But what makes these parables so forcible, is that they are not merely parables we can grasp, but parables we must enact. That is why they get right in amongst us. He has given us the friendship of Father and Son, on a level of equality—*nihil in hac Trinitate vel maius vel minus*—as the clue to the most august of mysteries, the life of the Godhead. It is hard for us to worship the divine reality, if we are falsifying in our own person the human parable: if we are ungrateful or indifferent sons to our earthly fathers. I am so sorry for those of you who have to try to be otherwise; I never had to try at all. My little blind soul, nosing its way into the world, had been so careful in the choice of a father.

Farrer, *The End of Man*, pp. 67-69.

Mothers

My sisters and I were born in Hampstead, and were brought up by a mother who was so dependable, she was almost like a piece of God's nature herself. The house always went smoothly. There was very little money behind it, but somehow no one was allowed to feel the strain. There were always good meals on time—my mother got very tired, I believe, but she did it somehow. She soothed everyone's troubles and never mentioned her own. If she had made more fuss, I suppose I should have taken more notice: if I had had to do without her, I should have seen what I owed to her. Her goodness made me thoughtless. I remember once thinking it would be fun to drive home from Oxford with three fellow students, who were going far and so wanted to start very early. 'We'll stop at our place,' I said, 'and have breakfast.' I rang my mother up at some terrible hour in the morning and we all landed hungry on the mat. The breakfast was there and my mother smiled. It was only years afterwards that she recalled the occasion, and laughed at me for having been so absurd. She had had practically nothing in the larder.

And so it is the faithfulness of God, his unseen dependableness, which makes us ungrateful. 'Ah, my dear Mother,' I can now say, 'how I wish . . .'—but it is too late . . .

My mother was a good woman—no one more truly a Christian—and I dare say she did not specially want to be made a fuss of, or to hear endless speeches of thanks. She wanted her children to grow and thrive on her kindness, to work along with her efforts in bringing us up. There is a sort of unthankfulness which is far more cruel than an unthankful tongue—and that is, a contempt for people's services to us. Is a cook more hurt by our lack of praise, or by our leaving her food uneaten? The worst ungratefulness to parents is, not asking for their help, not taking their advice; if they give us presents of clothes, not wearing them; if they give us presents of books, not reading them.

So it is with God. The real unthankfulness is pushing away the things he wants to give us most. We accept the material benefits—the sunshine, the rain, the food, and all the powers of nature which he has taught us to use so skilfully. And certainly God wants to give us these things, and loves to see us enjoy them, just as our mother liked to see us eat. For all our happiness is dear to God, and especially if we share it with others and invite them to our table.

But there are things he wants even more to give us— so much so, that he sent his Son to die for us. He wants to give us—how can I say it?—he wants to give us himself. Sunshine and rain, food, drink and medicine will not keep us alive for more than some seventy or eighty years. If God shares his life with us, it will keep us alive for ever. But only if the life of God gets under our skins, and makes us divine. We have to grow together into one with Christ, for God is in Christ already . . .

Religion is all concerned with the faithfulness of God

and with the unfaithfulness of men. We lose heart in religion, because we think we can trust ourselves to be faithful to God. We break down and then we are discouraged. No, religion is not pretending to be faithful, it is trust in the faithfulness of God, and going back to him again and again and again for forgiveness and a fresh start.

So, then, we have come here to thank God for his goodness. But there is only one sort of thanks he cares for, and that is, that we should use his most precious gifts, and not despise what he died to give us. 'I've been dying to get to know you,' people sometimes say to a new acquaintance, and heaven knows what they mean. But Christ died to get to know us, or (since he knows us already) he died to bring us into fellowship with him. 'Behold', he says, 'I stand at the door and knock. If any man will open, I will come in, and share his supper; and he shall share mine.'

Farrer, The End of Man, pp. 54-56.

—THE USE OF MONEY—

Wasting Money

If we waste our money, we are not only guilty of wasting a talent which God has given us, we are not only guilty of making that useless which is so powerful a means of doing good, but we do ourselves this further harm, that we turn this useful talent into a powerful means of corrupting ourselves; because so far as it is spent wrong, so far it is spent in the support of some wrong temper, in gratifying some vain and unreasonable desires, in conforming to those fashions and pride of the world, which as Christians and reasonable men we are obliged to renounce . . .

For so much as is spent in the vanity of dress may be reckoned so much laid out to fix vanity in our minds. So much as is laid out for idleness and indulgence may be reckoned so much given to render our hearts dull and sensual . . .

So that on all accounts, whether we consider our fortune as a talent and trust from God, or the great good that it enables us to do, or the great harm that it does to ourselves if idly spent, on all these great accounts it appears that it is absolutely necessary to make reason and religion the strict rule of using all our fortune.

Law, *A Serious Call*, pp. 98-99.

A Way to Make Amends

What a large stock would the poor have to the fore, if Christians would but lay by for them all that they lay out in unnecessaries: nay, if they were but to have all that Christians lay out in sin and vanity, in pride, intemperance, etc., to comply with evil customs, etc.! And, in good truth, I cannot see how any Christian can make amends, such as will be accepted of God, for all his idle expenses; but by giving to the poor in some way proportionable to the money he has misspent, and what he has by him.

Wilson, *Maxims*, p. 13.

Give

Give, looking for nothing again, that is, without consideration of future advantages: give to children, to old men, to the unthankful, and the dying, and to those you shall never see again: for else your alms or curtesy is not charity, but traffick and merchandise: and be sure that you omit not to relieve the needs of your enemy and the injurious; for so possibly you may win him to your self; but do you intend the winning him to God.

Taylor, *Holy Living*, p. 229.

Money Is Opportunity

It is good to give riches away—not because money is a bad thing: charity isn't like the hot penny in the children's game, which you pass on as fast as you can from hand to hand, since you are to lose a forfeit if you are caught holding it. No, the reason against holding much money is that money is power, money is opportunity, and your poor neighbours haven't got enough of it. Money is a serious subject. There is nothing more bogus than that affectation of aristocratic high-mindedness which considers the weighing of expenses to be beneath notice, and the paying of tailors' bills to be a bourgeois scruple.

Farrer, *The End of Man*, p. 82.

The Rich Man

[The rich man] will not . . . look at the lives of Christians, to learn how he ought to spend his estate, but he will look into the scriptures and make every doctrine, parable, precept, or instruction that relates to rich men a law to himself in the use of his estate.

Law, *A Serious Call*, p. 59.

—— DISCERNMENT ——

Perceptiveness

I had five aunts who lived together in a Hampstead house known to their nephews and nieces as the Aunt-Heap. They were extremely charitable, and never was there a household of people who so consistently bought cabbages from bad greengrocers because their wives suffered from varicose veins, or employed slatternly char-women because their husbands were supposed to be reclaimed drunkards. Their numerous fringe of casual employees were known by us collectively as the Old Frauds. One object of their charity was an indigent cousin of some kind who was bedridden. If you visited her you would sooner or later—and a good deal sooner than later—hear her tale of woe. A doctor had recommended the amputation of her leg at the knee and promised to set her upright on a wooden peg. 'But', said cousin Harriet, 'that very night the Holy Ghost said to me, "Miss Barker, don't you have it off."' With the result that she was useless to herself, and a care to others, for the remaining forty years of her life. No doubt an edifying conclusion.

We will now get on the time machine and come some forty years nearer to the present day. A young woman joined an enthusiastic religious group which ran like wildfire round the world in the twenties and thirties. In the solvent atmosphere of a shared emotion she fell in love with a man formerly of bad life whom the group had converted. But just as the wedding began to look like practical politics she was seized with terrible misgivings. Did the man genuinely love her and would it last? She made the mistake of sharing her anxiety with the group, with which, indeed, she was taught to share all things. Theirs was a meeting of communal quiet. They laid it before the Lord and they waited for guidance. The leader uttered the oracle; and it was the current saying in the group, that the leader's guidance was always right. The spirit declared that the marriage was to go forward. The girl's fears were groundless. It was a marriage in the Lord, it would consecrate their union with the fellowship and keep them steadfast in the Lord's work. Very edifying; but the husband quickly relapsed into his evil life, cursed the Christian group with all his heart, brought his mistresses into his house, and drove out his two children and his wife. The woman, being brave and steadfast, worked and brought up her children. So the human race got two recruits out of the mess, for it is God's way to bring his good out of our evil. I find it hard to believe, however, that the evil was the intention of his holy will in the first place.

The two cases I've narrated to you are both true fact, and the comparison between them is instructive. Old cousin Harriet followed her heart: the young woman went against hers. What hit cousin Harriet with the force of divine authority was something which came rushing up from the bottom of her mind, and I could put a name to it— so could you—it was animal fear, the fear of the surgeon's knife. What overbore the unlucky young bride was group support for the leader's ideas; and his ideas did not come so much from the heart, as from the head. The reason why the group held that Dick's guidance was always right was that he had an uncanny skill in planning an evangelistic campaign, so as to obtain visible success in the short run. And so, I suppose, he was doing in the case of this unfortunate engagement of marriage. He was, as was habitual with him, seeing it as part of his group tactics. Marriages within the group tended to hold the group together; and especially to tie in a man of popular gifts, a potentially useful agent of propaganda who was, however, dangerously unstable. So he sacrificed the individual to the collective plan, like any communist.

58

So, the one case the heart seized control, in the other the head. What, then, was the matter? We know very well that we've got to listen to our heart, and also to our head; there's no folly in attending to either. The common error in the two cases was simply a mistaken belief in inspiration. You could not argue with cousin Harriet's fear, and what was worse, she couldn't argue with it herself. For she must not resist the Holy Ghost, lest she be found to be fighting against God. And so with Dick's guidance: once it was acclaimed as the voice of God, it was irresistible. The young lady should have been free to say: I see the force of Dick's view—it is perfectly true that marriages within the group are helpful to the group and to its evangelistic work, but only if these marriages are sound. Now as to whether this marriage in particular is sound, neither Dick nor any other member of the group is so well placed for judging as I am. It is I who feel the quality of the man's attitude to me and it fills me with a misgiving which no amount of argument can quiet or dispel.

The trouble about an indiscreet belief in inspiration is that it smothers reason. A man who declares 'This is what the Spirit directs' is not required to give a reason; surely God does not argue his cases. But I say to you, always suspect claims to inspired guidance which bypass reasoned argument. There are not fewer reasons for what God ordains than for other things; there are more, far more. There are all the reasons in the world, if we can but find them. For is not he wise?

If I were sitting where you sit, and hearing the preacher produce these old skeletons out of the family cupboard, I think that I should be saying something like this. 'The man is talking common sense and flat worldly wisdom, and I wouldn't want to dispute it on that level. Only what he is saying amounts to this—that the Christian Gospel isn't true, but quite false. For the Gospel promises us the Holy Spirit to guide us; whereas the preacher says that no belief can be more dangerous than the belief that we have the guidance of the Spirit.' If, in fact, any of you are sharing any such protest as that, I agree that it's a perfectly fair challenge and as such I propose to take it up.

Is the Christian inspired? Yes, he is indeed. Just as inspired as he is Christian, and just as Christian as he is inspired. Are we not told that the Spirit is Christ's other self and that the Spirit in us is the very overflow of Christ's divine life? And, as St. Paul says, putting it negatively, those that are not led by the Spirit of Christ are none of his, that is, they are not Christians at all. Only *how* does the Spirit of Christ shape our spirits? I am going, in answer, to give you a very dull word, a word which has no poetic colour or emotional aura—the word is, attitude. The Christian who seeks in prayer and sacrament the company of Christ, who puts himself into the acts and concerns of Christ, is drawn quite without consciousness, perhaps, into the attitudes of Christ. And Christ's attitude is a two-sided relationship: to his divine Father, and to his human brothers. The so-called Christian virtues are attitudes—Christ's attitudes passing over into us, to become ours. Attitudes, for example, of faith, of hope, of love. These attitudes, so far as we Christians share them, are simply Christlike, simply divine, and no inspiration we could possibly receive could be higher or diviner than this. There is nothing better, in this life, that God could give us.

The attitudes are the basic things, the immediate form of the divine life in us. But then, of course, they carry with them many particular illuminations. The mind governed by Christ's faith, Christ's hope, Christ's love, is the mind that sees straight, and so the convert cries with the blind man healed in the Gospel story: 'I was blind; and now I see!' Of course conversion to Christ brings spiritual perceptiveness: for it teaches us to look through the eyes of God!

Between getting one's spiritual eyes, and claiming oracular inspirations, the difference is wide. Oracular assurances are a *substitute* for intellectual sight, whereas what we are talking about is a clearing of intellectual sight. A good pair of spectacles is not a substitute for the use of one's eyes. When I have the advantage of spectacles, I do not say, 'My spectacles tell me so-and-so', but, 'I see such-and-such a state of affairs'. My spectacles do not inform me, they make my sense perfect, so that the visible world may inform me. The Christian mind quickened by faith, hope and love is simply capable of a greater perceptiveness. Heaven help the Christian whose prayers do not make him quicker of eye to appreciate another's need, and to hear the call of duty as it arises in every circumstance of life! The Christian whose prayers make him more shut up in himself, less open to the glory of the world or to the image of God in his fellows, what sort of a Christian is he? And to what can he be praying? Surely to wood or stone, and not to the living God, the Father of our Lord Jesus Christ.

We say in the Creed, I believe in the Holy Ghost, the lifegiver, who spoke through the prophets. The two functions are one. How did he speak through the prophets? How else than by making them all alive? And when they were alive, then they were alive to what surrounded them, and alive to what God was doing and declaring in their days, and so what they saw they could not but speak.

Well, this is very fine, and if God did not more for us than make us divinely alive to himself and to one another, we might think he had done all we would dare to ask. But does not he do more? Does he not (for all I may say) give his servants special inspiration, showing them things about their call or their destiny which they could never gather from looking round on the world, never mind with how clear or enlightened eyes? Well, yes, he does. I will fish another rag out of my family dustbin for you—a very commonplace example. There was my little old aunt Ellen. She did not join the Aunt-Heap until long after cousin Harriet's time—not until she was old. Till then she had somewhere else to be, and something else to do. She was the tiniest creature—as small as a mouse, and as timid. In her girlhood she fainted at every sight of blood. But steadily through her teens the conviction grew in her that Christ would have her go to India as a missionary doctor. Not that there were any missionary doctors of her sex then; the medical schools only opened to women in the year she was ready to enter. So she went—and I will not enlarge on the story of her life. I will merely say that if we can be voted into Paradise by the voices of the poor, my little aunt will have had an easy passage. But all that's irrelevant. I have only to speak now of her resolution, or conviction about her calling, slowing maturing in patience and fidelity, with no excitement, no tension, no oracles from the skies, but a growing sense of what God meant to make of her, and through her. And so, perhaps, God will give you assurance of the calling he has for you; and this, I say, is a manner of inspiration which goes somewhat beyond the mere sharpening of our eyes to see what is around us.

Just now I gave you a word: attitude. And now I will give you another—depth. The sharing of the Lord's attitude of heart and mind through prayer is not just Yes or No—you either share it or you don't—it's a matter of depth. We can enter deeply, or shallowly, into the divine-human life of Christ.

Farrer, *The End of Man*, pp. 62-66.

Should I?

The [spiritual] director is not there to instruct people what to do, but may often help them to greater awareness of all the factors involved: e.g.

1) Is the proposed action loving? (The famous words inscribed at Mahatma Gandhi's place of cremation may sometimes be relevant: "Recall the face of the poorest and the most helpless man whom you have seen, and ask yourself if the step you contemplate is going to be of any use to him. Will he be able to gain anything by it? Will it restore him to control over his own life and destiny?")

2) How does the proposed action respond to our *reasoning* about it?

3) How do others, whose views we respect, feel about it?

4) Does it impinge favourably or unfavourably upon the basic direction of Scripture or any major traditions of the Church?

5) What will be the consequences of acting or not acting in this way?

6) How far has the person prayed about the decision?

Jeff, *Spiritual Direction*, p. 41.

Nothingness

Screwtape to Wormwood:

You can make him [the patient] waste his time not only in conversation he enjoys with people whom he likes but also in conversations with those he cares nothing about, on subjects that bore him. You can make him do nothing at all for long periods. You can keep him up late at night, not roistering, but staring at a dead fire in a cold room. All the healthy and outgoing activities which we want him to avoid can be inhibited and *nothing* given in return, so that at last he may say, as one of my own patients said on his arrival down here, "I now see that I spent most of my life in doing *neither* what I ought *nor* what I liked." The Christians describe the Enemy as one "without whom Nothing is strong." And Nothing is very strong: strong enough to steal away a man's best years not in sweet sins but in a dreary flickering of the mind over it knows not what and knows not why, in the gratification of curiosities so feeble that the man is only half aware of them, in drumming of fingers and kicking of heels, in whistling tunes that he does not like, or in the long, dim labyrinth of reveries that have not even lust or ambition to give them a relish, but which, once chance association has started them, the creature is too weak and fuddled to shake off.

Lewis, *The Screwtape Letters*, pp. 555-56.

Night Cometh

St. John (i,5) says that Christ is a light in the darkness of this world, a light which the darkness never overtook—

not, I think, never *comprehended*, as our old version has it: that is not the point in this place. In a sense, Christ was as much overtaken as any of us, by nightfall and the striking hour. Very often, we must suppose, since he was the type of that good Samaritan, who turned aside from his scheduled journeys to heed the cry of need. Darkness overtook him, he fell short of his inn, and camped by the wayside. And yet, it did not *overtake* him, as an alien thing: for he was himself, says St. John, the Word by whom the world was made, and through whom light and darkness were both appointed. He was no more *overtaken* by the darkness, than I am *overtaken* by the words I freely speak. His earthly mission, his charitable action, were one with the cycles of the sun and moon; they all went together to compose the single but manifold purpose of God. He did not fret at the passage of time, it did not accuse him of negligence, nor did it mock him for his impotence. He had taught, he had healed, he had journeyed, he had prayed as the time allowed. That his planned journey should fail, all this was carried in the higher plan by which, human choice and heavenly providence concurring, he moved forward to the redemption of mankind, and the marriage of heaven with earth. He never watched time running through his fingers: when he still had more than thirty years in hand, he spent them at a single throw, and bought the pearl of infinite price. You can say that, in the end, he embraced darkness: he never let it overtake him.

When I was a boy, my father, wishing to encourage me at once in Greek and in handicraft, and to edify himself at the same time, caused me to carve him a little wooden plaque, with the words, *ERCHETAI NUX*, night cometh; the night, that is, in which no man can work. And this he put under the clock in his study, to discourage him from idleness, a warning, it seems to me, he of all men least needed; and yet, when he came to the end of his life, he would lament how little he had made of it. And so we are all likely to feel. Time accuses us, time, and those awful words, 'We have left undone what we ought to have done'—for God knows what that is. And when we are most triumphant in the sense of having overtaken time, and imposed our achievement on the day, we may have most cause to rue, in our supposed success, the failure to have done the only thing that would have been truly worth while.

If we have to suppose that any souls are condemned to everlasting misery, surely a striking clock will not be left out of the equipment of their prison; the sound of time relentlessly passing, and never occupied to the hearer's content. A life on earth continually overtaken by time, and by remorse, is a pattern of damnation: but if we suffer such a hell on earth, it is only for lack of taking hold upon the redemption so freely offered to us. The Light, which darkness overtaketh not has shined on our heads: he who commits his soul to Christ is one with the will which made both night and day. He puts himself into the hands of Christ, to live in his will. He will not be perfect, and so he will have many repentances for time misspent; but he will be humble and believing, therefore he will feel no remorse. He will say: I missed this or that call from a fellow-being, I followed my pride, or my pleasure, I did not do as you, my Lord, would have done. But you have let me fall into these errors to show me my heart, and you, in your mercy, will use them for my discipline, and turn them to account in the designs of your loving kindness. You have undertaken my life, and you will bring it to good. While we are yours, we shall never be overtaken by darkness; work out in us the purpose of your perfect will and bring us to that day, which will marry us to joy, and ring every peal in all the city of heaven.

Farrer, *A Celebration of Faith*, pp. 190-192.

Resisting the Current

It is a sickly age of infidelity, which has not only deprived us of religion, but of common sense, and of the common faculty of thinking. A foolish generation: It is a certain sign of a sound and steady virtue and judgment, not to be carried along with the current of libertinism and infidelity. Let us make this wise choice, to be happy with the few, rather than to go to hell with the crowd.

Wilson, *Maxims*, p. 74.

—ACKNOWLEDGMENTS—

Excerpt from Donne, *The Sermons of John Donne*, edited by George R. Potter and Evelyn M. Simpson. 10 volumes. Berkeley, Calif.: University of California Press, 1953-62. Copyright © 1953-1962 Regents. Reprinted by permission.

Excerpt from Farrer, *The Brink of Mystery*, edited by Charles C. Conti. London: SPCK, 1976. Reprinted by permission of the publisher.

Excerpts from Farrer, *A Celebration of Faith*. London: Hodder and Stoughton, Ltd., 1970. Reprinted by permission of the publisher.

Excerpts from Farrer, *The End of Man*, 1973. Reprinted by permission of SPCK.

Excerpts from Farrer, *A Faith of Our Own*, 1960. Reprinted by permission of the Honorable Penelope Piercy, for Trust of Mrs. K.D. Farrer deceased.

Excerpt from Farrer, *God Is Not Dead*, 1966. Reprinted by permission of Morehouse Publishing Company.

Excerpt from Farrer, *Love Almighty and Ills Unlimited*. Garden City, N.Y.: Doubleday, 1961. Reprinted by permission of Doubleday, a division of Bantam Doubleday Dell Publishing Group Inc.

Excerpt from Jeff, *Spiritual Direction for Every Christian*. London: SPCK, 1987. Reprinted by permission of the publisher.

Excerpts from Law, *A Serious Call to a Devout and Holy Life*, edited by Paul G. Stanwood. Copyright © 1978. Reprinted by permission of the Paulist Press.

—OTHER WORKS QUOTED—

More, Hannah. *Christian Morals.* In vol. 2 of *The Works of Hannah More.* New York, 1848.

———. *Practical Piety.* Burlington, N.J., 1811.

Pusey, Edward Bouverie. *Spiritual Letters of Edward Bouverie Pusey. . .*London, 1898.

Wilson, Thomas. *Maxims of Piety and of Christianity.* Edited by Frederic Relton. London, 1898.